MARE NOSTRUM

Khaled Mattawa

Quarternote Chapbook Series #16

Sarabande Books
Louisville, KY

Library of Congress Cataloging-in-Publication Data

Names: Mattawa, Khaled, author.
Title: Mare nostrum : poems / Khaled Mattawa.
Description: First edition. | Louisville, KY : Sarabande Books,
[2019] |
Series: Quarternote chapbook series
Identifiers: LCCN 2018030468 | ISBN 9781946448361 (print)
Classification: LCC PS3563.A8387 A6 2019 | DDC 811/.54--dc23
LC record available at https://lccn.loc.gov/2018030468

Interior and exterior design by Danika Isdahl.
cover image © Slim Fejjari, first published in "Erano come due
notti" © Else srl, Roma 2011

Manufactured in Canada.
This book is printed on acid-free paper.
Sarabande Books is a nonprofit literary organization.

This project is supported in part by an award from the
National Endowment for the Arts. The Kentucky Arts
Council, the state arts agency, supports Sarabande Books with
state tax dollars and federal funding from the National
Endowment for the Arts.

Traveler, where are you heading?
You embark, take sick and return.
So many innocents like you and me
were duped and lost their way.

Dahman El Harrach

Ours be the tossing—wild through the sea—
Rather than a mooring—unshared by thee.

Emily Dickinson

MARE NOSTRUM

Psalm of Departure

Locusts wrap the sun in gauze,
the river swallows its banks.
No pleasure but seeing the no-

king crop here, the no-fields,
a petrified forest where twins were slain.
Someone will follow a bird.

The work of fire never ends:
Djinn build cities of mirage,
the poor stand waiting by the shore.

Signs made of stardust and spider
thread. Any way you measure it,
the difference will be a road.

Season of Migration to the North/Northwest

Spent years gathering eucalyptus leaves
from King Menelik's forests—their fire
makes the best injera, I'm told.

You climb wheezing, choking
on Addis air, then you find yourself
in these scented woods.

Back breaking, but I love bundling
the leaves, how the rain soaks
the scent into your clothes and skin.

Maybe that's why Menelik built
his palace here, a great church looming
over it to show he was content.

But even he was tempted away;
his queen sent a messenger from the foot
of Entoto saying she's found a new *addis*

flower *ababa* and he followed her
like Adam out of paradise
to cofound the metropolis nightmare.

Was my dream worth more than enough
air to live on, something between
banal sin and the creator's potency?

Addis to the source of the Nile,
then Khartoum to Sinai, to be
an asylee in Tel Aviv, or northwest

through Darfur and Sebha,
to the Bride of the Med.
Names like shabby trees on a map,

lines for a screen where bodies
are stick figures dancing
to tepid applause. Each a degree

in a circle inside a void, unmarked
time, days like scentless leaves
that slip through your hands.

Psalm on the Road to Agadez

Day and night traveled
to reach these shores
West to North

East to North
North to North
to North to North

your country,
your savage country
where you are free!

Psalm Under Siege

Speak the body's thrift, the blood
and breath sustained by a candle
flame, remembrances

encircle like moths. No seagulls
when fishermen return
empty-handed to Arwad.

Locust-ravaged Idlib's fields,
the dry wells of Daraa. Candle
light or soul—what else to call

what remains alive in me, how
it shrinks like irises blinded
by death's blazing noon.

Constance Song

Wave, checkpoint and dune—
the roads we tread.
Each day a ragged plastic cup

and people who forget how to die
the way loss befriends lament
to a fog heavy with wings.

"Far away, somewhere,
 I have a brother or a sister
 in this world," my Blessing hums.

Agadez Blues

No place, no money for the bed
Je dors dans la rue paid only the way
Even God can't see me here

Police take your money
quand tu n'as pas d'argent
even God can't hear me here

Ils te palpent tout le corps pour vérifier
palpent all your body
Even God can't save me here

I pay 1300 francs go to Libye
mais le chauffeur, il est parti
Even God can't help me here

Je n'ai plus rien pour manger
Je n'ai plus rien pour dormir
Even God can't find me here

Psalm for Crossing Nimroz

What is a mere grazer
to the world of the many
and contending,

to the jealous one
of this Earth's drying grass?
What to them? .

What to time and limb
spent this far, the wind
voracious, its mind aflame?

Psalm Under Siege

Speak the jet fighter's contrails,
speak the rumble of my pulse,
its screech and roar of barrel bombs.

A cesspool of sewer overflow
and a broken water main—a gleaming
lake haunting your thirst.

Reeds shoot up from its shores,
sununu hop in between, chirping
when the shellings pause.

Malouk's Ode

I tap a few words to her on WhatsApp or Viber
to blot out the day. I bring my nose close to the screen
to smell the photos she sends.

Selfies of her by the gas stove, or the baby making a gesture,
a smile or a yawn or cry. Sometimes a video of an old song.
She asks about the sea; it's calm but the traffickers no show.

She breaks me, a softness that turns me dusk,
I, the poet dissident who labored to rephrase
with healing the nations' inflamed contract,

who roved the bone sculptures made governments,
the sanctuaries filled fear bright eyes,
my words now monosyllabic soft as sighs.

There was blindness in my game, my epic of home.
I hear the smugglers, their pupils shifting as if following
a maddened gull, some bootleg spasm and discharge.

A blindness that cannot stop seeing,
those eyes will keep shifting like this in their graves.
I see my spirit too, a plastic cloud drifting in the breeze.

With them is our last chance, for what?
From the village drying up to sand, the town without jobs,
the hands that never learned to write, the eyes that barely read,

the soul hunger stump and trade.
Am I writing my poem again?
Have I become the exile I so mock and detest?

How to walk this sea?
How to not believe that such is possible?
Arrived in Kufra, the cramped 4x4s,

the Hilux where spent bodies cling to wooden poles,
Ivecos, hundred-packed swaying death's wave.
Emptied in the camp, divided between sheets of galvanize,

the courtyard littered, bottles, clothes, old photographs
like some carnival bacchanal the night before,
a town facing massacre just fled.

An empty once-crowded barracoon
where the signal is one ribbon strong.
It is from here that I send her all my love.

Blessing's Song

The hands of your
kin, pits of desire
for the pain of others, O poet friend?

Flogging pounding
prodding scalding
human flesh, O poet friend?

Is this the legacy
of your noble
long-awaited revolt, O poet friend?

The Affari

Someone reaping land, trading it
for a 4x4 or a shipload of gasoline,
each body delivered or shipped.

Something to the trafficker, rescue worker, boat mechanic,
truck driver, salesman, food exporter, tire repairman,
money changer, doctor, medicine man, volunteer.

For each house torn down or blown
up, each bullet-riddled school, each
clinic built, detention center overran.

Something to peace-
keeper, terrorist, jet-
drone bombing him.

A salary, a bribe
a grant, a stipend
a ransom, a fellowship.

Into the Sea

Barely out of the jetty, the boat rises
with every wave, and in the back
2 or 3 fall into the sea.

At sunset the boat starts to lose
air, fills with water, mothers
and babies fall into the sea.

One side stays afloat. We cling
to a rope, water up to our belly
and people fall into the sea.

All night we grip and bleed.
Rain so cold, waves 5 stories high.
If only I could fall into the sea.

Sunrise, a helicopter. I find
a red shirt, wave it to them.
They watch us fall into the sea.

They fling a small inflatable boat,
I am too weak to reach it.
Others try and fall into the sea.

A cargo boat throws a rope,
get us on board. Alive at last,
and we still fall into the sea.

With Lines Taken from Walt Whitman

The auctioneer in militia fatigues,
pushes you aside to conduct his business.
He has twelve lined up:

of the bonds, fees, threats
and the quintillion beneficiaries,
the revolving cycle of birth,

poverty and abuse,
truly and steadily roll'd:
he knows nothing, or pretends;

or how they ended up in his hands,
and whence they go—
only his small part in the trade.

And of the cunning tendons and nerves,
under the glare of searchlight beams—
how will they swim the pool of labor's excess?

What building site or garment floor?—
no time to be stript. Flakes of breast-muscle,
pliant backbone, good-sized arms and legs,

where they had been Tasered, slashed
and whipped: that you may see them—
nothing, or pretends.

But witness, you note how the living
eyes matte, the faces acumen-stripped.
"Brothers, we have no time," he says.

Spare him talk of countless immortal lives
in parlors and lecture-rooms
across rich republics and Frontex states.

He knows within there runs blood,
same old blood! How easily it spills,
how evidence is hid and drained.

Whatever the bids of the bidders,
none of your brothers
will exceed a 100 quid.

Psalm for the Balkan Route

At peace in the palm: embers,
perfumes, the scents of Abyssinia
and Mecca haunt the brain.

You remember weddings and feasts.
Hail pocked the copper dust, and you,
opened mouthed, gazed at the world.

Years have passed since that since.
How does the body know how to pin
so much of itself in words?

Song for Amadou

Have you made it
to Sicily, Amadou?
Are you deep

in the woods of Denmark?
Learned a new language,
writing your book?

Have they put you on
a plane home, Amadou?
Kidnapped you, sent you back

to that camp in Bani Walid,
slaving day and night
on a farm for some crook.

Are you in paradise
now, Amadou?
A skeleton bleaching

in the sand,
a bloated corpse
on a sunny beach.

Trafficker Monologue

Don't fear their eyes. They came
to you, after all, they paid their way.
Oh, they'll kill you given the chance.

You are a key in the dicey maze of
their lives, you clamp the cruelest lock.
Your breath is as foul as theirs.

Sometimes you think you'd had enough
of this trade in death, so much life,
these knots of unsorted dreaming.

But the sea is calm again, bats circle
the tangerine grove, riding the sultry breeze.
Time to send another boat, perhaps.

What's her name? Constance or
Blessing, the one paying her fare in bed—
she'll be here when you return.

Fuel Burns

Gasoline canisters leak
or get knocked over;
gasoline mixes with seawater,

and when the mixture
touches human skin,
skin begins to burn.

Women sitting in the bottom
or the center of the boat
are at highest risk.

Dinghies are fitted
with plywood floors
fixed with nails and screws

that puncture people's feet.
The wood soaks up water,
expands, and then splits.

Women and children often
fall through the floor
or are trampled, and drown.

People fight on the boat,
the bodies of survivors
and the dead are full

of scratches, bite marks,
cuts and bruises but it's
fuel burns that horrify most.

Survivors arrive
hypothermic, dehydrated,
barely conscious.

They must shower
with soap to get relief,
and need help stripping off

their fuel-soaked clothes,
but just touching their clothing
can make latex gloves melt.

This poem is an erasure from a blog entry by Dr. Sarah Giles, a Canadian
physician who volunteered for Doctors Without Borders in the Central
Mediterranean in 2016.

Malouk's Qassida

Lampedusa a 100 leagues now, the bay
between it and Sousse a corridor of debris,
a Phoenician graveyard.

Are we prepared for the storm's paradise?
The starlings recite the zodiacs on their wings;
the marabouts must in kindness abide.

On the wireless the noises of rescue—
a blank of unconsciousness and disuse—
into a theater of salvation we ride.

We are exalted into some hippopotamus,
our mouths checked, hands gloved
with inhuman skin, their fingers inside.

The mouths that speak covered like the Tuaregs',
their eyes swathed with a dusky mirage.
Our names, taken, flicker like fireflies.

Looped around our wrists, numbers
that look like a kind of price.
The bullhorns cry, the seagulls deride.

On the bridges to those slippery worlds, we are
wrapped in gold foil, disease-free. Who is saving whom?
The question's not stated, only implied.

Psalm for Arrival

When we find the sounds
for words we need, their death
rattle begins to echo in our throats.

Memory creeps up on old sentiments,
finds them lurking like blind fish
in the twilight of our blood,

dead and living on—ancient prophesies
or frozen microbes—something we disavow,
but that continues to feed on us.

Moria Refugee Camp Journal

about you
a grave
yard

on this
much
that

—the that—
you live
in

—the this
much—you
live on

the all
about you
a grave

a yard or
two—the
not much

the yes,
you are
one too

'Allams for Robert Hayden

wind hurtles us
   dinghy bundles
      blood fever

our languages
   falling into
      unsure

we as your own
   prophet of love
      your hands

was it discipline
   or self-love
      brought us

a number
   a listing
      a teenager

dead whales
   breaking
      gills catch

pray for death
   wet oblivion
      of corpses

we who survive
   rescue us
      reroute us

sacrifice
   a bleary rain
      insolvent

a bathroom wall
   some webpage
      prostitute

breaker-flung
   apart spilling us
      panic's oxygen

like stone
   souls rising
      to reclaim

prophet of hope
   into jubilance
      into labor's clock

self-hate
   a harmattan
      to these shores

in Palermo
   Allah is great
      Jesus is love

'Allams are a sequence of short poems chanted by the Bedouins of eastern Libya and western Egypt. The 'allam poems are composed to relay the poet's immediate circumstances, including conflict, economic hardship and lost love.

Psalm of the Volunteer
for the village of Skala Sikamineas

Dear world,
who am I
to condemn you

Dear eyes,
who am I
to blind you

Dear lies,
who am I
to chastise you

Dear hypocrisy,
who I am to claim
not to know you

Dear indignance,
who am I
to possess you

Dear ignorance,
who am I
to float above you

Dear soul,
Who am I
To shun you

Dear soul,
who am I
to shelter you

Dear soul,
how am I
to repair you

Qassida to the Statue of Sappho in Mytelini

Kyria, why do you stand askance, facing neither
        sea nor mountain,
not even toward your wildflower fields?

And the lyre on your shoulder, was it meant
        to be the size
of the plastic jugs shouldered by Moria's refugees?

I saw them in Sicily too, home of your exile,
        where no rescue
could pause time grating at their memories.

Your island is empty of poets, Kyria. I came
        to meet them,
to recall the trembling earth under my feet.

Hangers-on reporting to newsletters throng
        the cafés, researchers
hacking at fieldwork, polishing CVs.

The migrants are all court poets now. At night
        they labor to translate
their traumas into EU legalese.

Or sit at your feet shouting into cell phones
        to scattered relatives,
trying to crack the code of the model asylee.

Kyria, there's no way for me to see you, no date,
        or sculptor's name,
only fascist graffiti below your knees.

Why do your eyes glare lifeless like apricot pits,
        your stone body dim,
a paper lamp trembling in the breeze?

Is that you now, Kyria, holding Cleis's hand,
        wearing hijab,
glad to be home again, not quite at ease?

Psalm for the Departed

A fistful of myrrh in his left
hand, and his right's wave
is the Bennu's upward flight.

His voice a thread buried
in sand, a fluorescent light
inflaming a sky gleaming

with ink. He'll be pure and I will
stand, an inexplicable glyph
waiting to be assigned.

Measure now your heart's
contraband—all that's delved
between us. Measure it

in blood. Tell the mind to
withstand what it's discounted
but could not ever disavow.

Acknowledgments

I would like to thank the MacArthur Foundation and the University of Michigan for their generous support of my work. Some of these poems were written or revised during a residency at the University of Arizona Poetry Center.

I wish also to thank the editors of these magazines where some of the poems in this manuscript have been published or are forthcoming.

Iowa Review: "Psalm on the Road to Agadez," "Constance Song," "Constance Song," "Blessing's Song," "The Affari," "Trafficker Soliliquoy."

Kenyon Review: "Malouk's Ode," "Qassida to the Statue of Sappho in Mytelini," "Fuel Burns," "Moria Refugee Camp Journal," "Psalm of the Volunteer."

Artful Dodge: "Psalm Under Siege," "Psalm for Crossing Nimroz," "Psalm for the Balkan Route."

Making Mirrors: Writing/Righting by and for Refugees, edited by Jehan Bseiso and Becky Thompson (Interlink Press, 2019): "Psalm for Arrival."

New England Review: "Malouk's Qassida," "Psalm for the Departed."

Arkansas International: "Psalm of Departure," "Agadez Blues," "Psalm Under Siege (1)," "Psalm Under Siege (2)."

Fifth Wednesday: "Season of Migration to the North/Northwest," "Into the Sea," "Song for Amadou."

Khaled Mattawa currently teaches in the graduate creative writing program at the University of Michigan. He is the author of four books of poetry, and a critical study of the Palestinian poet Mahmoud Darwish. Mattawa has coedited two anthologies of Arab American literature and translated many volumes of contemporary Arabic poetry. His awards include the Academy of American Poets Fellowship prize, the PEN Award for Poetry in Translation, and a MacArthur Fellowship.

The Quarternote Chapbook Series honors some of the most distinguished poets and prose stylists in contemporary letters and aims to make celebrated writers accessible to all.

Sarabande Books is a nonprofit literary press located in Louisville, KY. Founded in 1994 to champion poetry, short fiction, and essay, we are committed to creating lasting editions that honor exceptional writing. For more information, please visit www.sarabandebooks.org.